GUY DE LA BÉDOYÈRE, MA

Books are   ＇ ¹ on or before
        ·¹   ＼ ⌄.

SAMIAN WARE

GW00670522

)GY

Cover photograph
A fragment of a Dragendorff 37 bowl made by the
Drusus I workshop at Les Martres-de-Veyre in Central
Gaul *c.* AD 100-25. From Billingsgate, London.
(Author's collection.)

British Library Cataloguing in Publication Data available.

Published by
SHIRE PUBLICATIONS LTD
Cromwell House, Church Street, Princes Risborough,
Aylesbury, Bucks HP17 9AJ, UK

Series Editor: James Dyer

ISBN 0 85263 930 9

First published 1988

Set in 11 point Times and printed in Great Britain by
C. I. Thomas & Sons (Haverfordwest) Ltd,
Press Buildings, Merlins Bridge, Haverfordwest, Dyfed.

Contents

4

List of illustrations

Preface and acknowledgements

The most common high-quality pottery used in Roman Britain was Gaulish samian ware, a bright red fine ware manufactured during the first two centuries AD in a huge range of forms, some of which were elaborately decorated. It is found on excavations of Roman sites in large quantities and, as a result of a great deal of specialist research, the pottery is comparatively well understood. This book is intended to help student and layman realise its importance to the archaeology of Roman Britain.

The samian industry was a complex one and many aspects remain obscure. Condensing the subject inevitably means that much must be omitted. It is to be hoped that this book will help point the student in the direction of further study and interest the layman in what was undoubtedly a remarkable phenomenon. Unlike some subjects in archaeology the samian industry is filled with the names of real individuals whose colossal output testifies to their skill and range of production.

As far as possible an example of everything discussed has been illustrated. An attempt has been made to describe the appearance of typical samian fabrics but these are only for guidance. Such descriptions are very subjective: fabric colour and type are affected by incorrect kiln-firing, soil conditions and burning.

Thanks are due to the following for their assistance: Catherine Johns of the British Museum, who read the text and helped with the selection of photographs; Peter Webster of University College, Cardiff; Joanna Bird; Christopher St John Breen of the Dartford and District Archaeological Group; the Fairlawne Estate, which allowed the Cinnamus bowl from Sedgebrook, excavated by the Kent Archaeological Society, to be photographed; and Philip Clarkstone, who photographed the items from the author's collection and the Sedgebrook bowl.

1. A group of samian vessels, showing some of the most important types. Top row: Dr 33 cup, Dr 45 mortarium, Dr 27 cup. Second row: two Dr 29 bowls (first century). Third row: two Dr 37 bowls, mid to late second century. Bottom row: Dr 30 bowl and Déchelette 72 vase, mid to late second century. (Copyright: British Museum.)

1
Introduction

In the late nineteenth century J. Collingwood Bruce wrote in his celebrated *Handbook to the Roman Wall* that: 'Pottery usually forms an abundant class of Roman relics in every camp that has been long occupied. The Samian ware is very beautiful, and very characteristic. It is sometimes embossed . . . but more frequently plain. This species of "ware" has been imported from the continent.'

The attraction of samian to antiquarians is obvious. It has always invited comment because of its quality and its decoration. This volume is primarily concerned with what Collingwood Bruce called 'embossed' samian ware (better known nowadays as 'decorated' samian ware) with a view to bridging a gap between specialist publications and site reports and other introductory works. Samian ware was mostly manufactured in Roman Gaul and forms part of a general class of Roman pottery: the red-gloss fine tablewares which include Arretine ware and African red slip ware amongst others. It was highly prized in antiquity as Pliny the Elder remarked in his *Natural History* (Book 35, chapter 160).

In recent years there has been an academic swing towards coarse wares, and rightly so; these innumerable local forms of pottery can tell us much about trade routes and the markets of Roman Britain yet were largely ignored until the 1950s. The products of the Gaulish samian kilns are relatively well known and there has been an assumption that samian is a familiar subject requiring little explanation. As a result plain samian is often discussed in excavation reports in the form of an unillustrated listing of types. This may be acceptable to the specialist but does little to help the student or interested layman understand why the samian is being reported.

Samian's importance to Romano-British archaeology is that it is found on most first- and second-century sites and can be dated with a degree of accuracy unusual for pottery. This is for two reasons. In the period concerned Roman Britain experienced a considerable amount of upheaval as the Roman army strove to reduce the island to a governable state in the face of strenuous opposition on the part of many of the inhabitants, as was recorded by Roman historians. In some cases inscriptions make it possible to assign absolute dates to these periods of warfare or associated events such as the construction of Hadrian's Wall in c.119-25. Samian found in the primary levels of the forts on Hadrian's Wall, but not, say, on forts of a generation before, can for the most part be assumed to be from workshops operating at around that time. The second reason is that the workshops which produced decorated samian tended to do so in their own individual styles, or at least in a general style of the period, and often stamped their names on the bowls or the moulds in which they were made. Specialist work has made it possible to recognise styles of known potters even from quite small pieces, so examples in the same style found on an undated site can help date that site.

The presence of samian can help trace the advance of romanisation and is an indication of the extent of trade routes, the local demand for such products and the ability to pay for them.

The situation is not always that simple, however. Many workshops defy analysis; many samian bowls and sherds defy attribution. Being a relatively expensive product, decorated samian might not be broken and discarded until long after it was actually made or redeposited as rubbish was moved about; this is known as a residual deposit. This raises the question of how modern archaeology should use samian as a dating tool and as a measure of trade and romanisation in Roman Britain.

2
Manufacture

Samian was manufactured in a number of places in Gaul. The principal areas were what are now called South, Central and East Gaul (figure 2). Their mould-decorated products are stylistically distinct and were available at different times as far as the export market was concerned, but the whole production period is confined to the first and second centuries AD with East Gaulish activity continuing into the third century. The Gaulish samian industry is most remarkable for its extraordinary dominance of the market in the Western Empire despite the existence of similar industries in, for example, Spain and Italy. La Graufesenque and the other South Gaulish centres, which dominated the first century AD, grew out of the decline of the first-century BC Italian samian industry based at Arezzo and a number of other Italian centres, the products of which are known as Arretine ware. Its greatest period of activity was from about 30 BC to AD 20. Arretine is usually matt red in contrast to Gaulish samian gloss and the vessels themselves have thinner walls. Decoration was usually of extremely high quality, reflecting the standards of decoration on metal vessels with which Arretine was no doubt in competition. Arretine ware is extremely rare in Britain because the industry had virtually died out by the time of the invasion.

Samian potteries

The reasons why certain places developed as samian pottery centres are not entirely clear but some can be suggested. Firstly, access to suitable clays must have played a part: the presence of the mineral illite in the clay seems to have been a factor. Secondly, the potteries needed good communications if they were to satisfy the export market. In the Roman world, because of the vast cost of road transport, this meant access to rivers and the sea. The South Gaulish centres were all on the Garonne river system (though limits of navigability here mean that roads must have been used to some extent), the Central Gaulish centres were on the Loire system and the East Gaulish centres were on the Rhine and Moselle (figure 2). However, the decline of some of these centres, despite these resources, shows that there must have been more factors behind initial success, such as labour costs, local politics and competition, but the details are lost to us.

These considerations are certainly likely to have been more

significant than known historical upheavals which are so often used to explain the rise and demise of organisations in antiquity. It is important to appreciate that very little is known about the organisation of samian potteries and this is likely to remain the case. Each workshop was probably completely different in its way of working, depending on the quite untraceable whims and idiosyncrasies of the participating individuals. Even the word 'workshop' is a useful catch-all term which fails to indicate whether one man, or fifty, was involved.

Name-stamps and signatures

The limited knowledge that does exist of samian workshop organisation is mostly derived from the practice of signing the products. The approximate period of a potter's working life can be deduced from analysing the find-spots of his products.

Potters' stamps and signatures take a number of forms (and should not be confused with 'graffiti', inscriptions placed on the vessels after firing; see below and chapter 9):

Bowl-stamps. These were name-stamps impressed into the bowl prior to firing. They may name the individual who made the bowl or the name of his employer. Generally the required letters were engraved into a die which, when pressed into the bowl, left an impression with raised letters (figure 3, *1-4*). These were the stamps used for plain bowls and can occur in a number of different places on the vessels but the centre of the floor is the most normal. Stamping plain vessels was not an invariable practice but most fall into this category.

Bowl-finishers' stamps. The stamps described above were also sometimes used on decorated bowls but they are rare. In this case they are called bowl-finishers' stamps and usually indicate that someone different from the mould-maker had produced the bowl. This is an important distinction because some bowl-finishers stamped bowls made in moulds of more than one style, suggesting that they purchased their moulds. Cintusmus was an Antonine Central Gaulish potter who made bowls from moulds by Cinnamus and Albucius. Normally such stamps occur in the centre of the floor on South Gaulish products, or on the outside of the bowl, rim or base, on Central Gaulish products.

Mould-makers' names. These occur on decorated bowls in two forms; the advertisement stamp and the hand-written signature. They were put on the mould but their impressions appeared on the bowls. It is important to realise that they name the style of the mould but not necessarily the maker of the bowl. As their

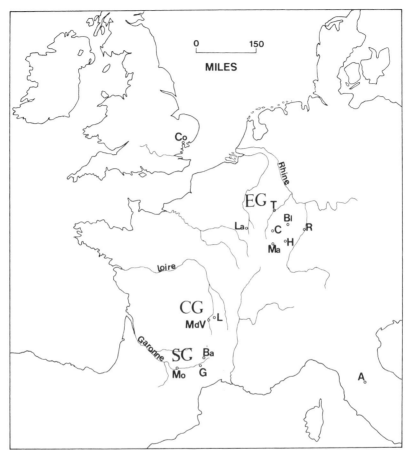

2. Samian manufacturing centres. Italy: A = Arezzo. South Gaul (SG): G = La Graufesenque, Ba = Banassac, Mo = Montans. Central Gaul (CG): MdV = Les Martres-de-Veyre, L = Lezoux. East Gaul (EG): R = Rheinzabern, T = Trier, La = Lavoye (Argonne), Ma = La Madeleine, Bl = Blickweiler, H = Heiligenberg. Britain: Co = Colchester.

significance was apparently to identify the mould they were usually the right way round on the mould. If so, they appear backwards, 'retrograde', on the bowl. Advertisement stamps appear as prominent features of the decoration and clearly they were meant to be seen on the finished product. They are most

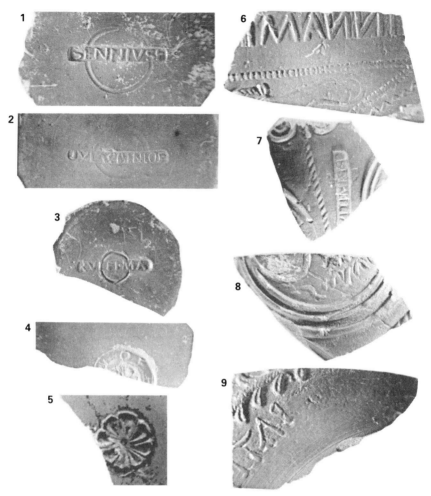

3. Samian potters' name-stamps. 1. SENNIUS.F, 'Sennius fecit', on an early second-century Dr 33 cup. 2. MACRINI.OF, 'the officina (workshop) of Macrinus', on a mid second-century Dr 33 cup. 3. RUFFI.MA, 'by the hand of Ruffus', on an early second-century Dr 33 cup. 4. Incomplete round stamp on a Dr 33 cup, showing the letters OF for 'officina'. 5. Anonymous rosette stamp on a late second-century dish. 6. Retrograde (backwards) advertisement stamp on a mid second-century Central Gaulish Dr 30 bowl showing the letters [C]INNAMI, 'of Cinnamus'. 7. Advertisement stamp on a late second-, early third-century East Gaulish Dr 37 bowl, showing the letters PRIMITIV[US]. 8. Late second-century Central Gaulish mould-maker's hand-written signature on the mould which has appeared on the bowl within the decoration, showing the letters SERVI[M], 'by the hand of Servus'. 9. Mid second-century Central Gaulish mould-maker's hand-written signature below the decoration, showing the letters PATE[RCLI], 'of Paterclus'.

common on Central and East Gaulish products of the mid second century and later (figure 3, *6-7*). Hand-written signatures are also known as 'cursive' signatures. They generally appear beneath the decorated zone and their impression on the bowl was usually obscured by the bowl-making process (figure 3, *8-9*). These are likely to have had significance only within the workshop, indicating the work of an employee. Cerealis signed his moulds which he had also stamped within the decoration with the name of Cinnamus, suggesting that he worked for Cinnamus. It is worth noting that in some cases if a potter bought a mould he might scratch his name on to it, though these are difficult to discern from a mould-signature put on before the mould was fired.

The potters' stamps take a number of grammatical forms. Some are a simple statement of name such as GEMINUS. Others indicate that the potter actually made the bowl by adding M or MA for *manu* ('by the hand of') or F or FEC for *fecit* ('made it'). For example, RUFFI.MA = 'by the hand of Ruffus' and SENNIUS.F = 'Sennius made it'. Such stamps seem to indicate that the named individual was personally responsible. Another form carries the abbreviation OF for *officina* ('workshop'), as in MACRINI.OF = 'the workshop of Macrinus'. This may mean that an anonymous employee was simply using the workshop stamp (figure 3, *1-4*).

Potters' stamps are by no means straightforward. There are thousands known and many potters used a number of variations of their names. It is quite usual for sherds to be broken across the name, leaving a potentially misleading suffix or prefix. As the stamp used a fraction of the space of decoration there is a much smaller chance that the surviving piece will bear the useful information of the stamp. Some potters were illiterate and used symbols, for example, a rosette (figure 3, *5*). Some potters had the same name as potters at work a century before. The only published reference book is now out of date and correct interpretation is only possible for experts who are familiar with the vast range of stamps so far recognised.

Another useful source of information is the collection of workshop tallies from La Graufesenque in South Gaul. These consist of dishes placed in kilns bearing potters' names and the numbers and types of vessels they had made. The information was scratched on to the dishes with a stylus. They show that in South Gaul tens of thousands of plain vessels might be fired simultaneously and that potters there shared kilns.

4. Basic samian vessel profiles used for moulded decoration. 1. Dr 11, the typical Arretine form. 2. Dr 29, in use up to *c.*85. 3. Dr 30, in use throughout the period. 4. Dr 37, *c.*70 and later. 5. Knorr 78, Flavian. 6. Déchelette 67, Flavian. 7. Déchelette 64. All to a scale of 1:8.

Bowl forms

Samian vessel forms have been classified by a number of specialists using their names and a number; the decorated forms most commonly encountered are known as Dragendorff (abbreviated to Dr) Forms 29, 30 and 37, Déchelette Form 67 and Knorr Form 78 (figures 4 and 5). All forms were made in South Gaul during the first century, though the 67 and 78 forms are always rare. In the second century, when the Central Gaulish factories held sway over the market, only forms Dr 30 and 37 were of significance. The most common Arretine decorated form, occasionally found in Britain, is the Dr 11 cup or crater (figure 4, *1*).

5. A group of unusual decorated forms. Left to right: Déchelette 67 jar, late first-century South Gaulish, height 8.1 cm; Déchelette 64 cup made by Libertus of Central Gaul, early second-century, height 9 cm; Knorr 78 bowl, late first-century South Gaulish, height 6.9 cm. (Copyright: British Museum.)

There were several different ways of decorating a samian bowl. In practice only certain forms received any decoration at all so the vast majority were plain. The most important method of decoration was that produced in moulds. This encouraged the development of individual styles because moulds allowed an almost infinite range of designs. The styles, coupled with fabric identification, make it possible to identify the products of separate workshops.

When discussing manufacture of these bowls it is important to remember that styles and design were established at the mould stage. We have no way of knowing how old a mould was when used to make bowls. Some were clearly worn; others may have sat around unused on workshop shelves. Equally, while the mould was often signed, especially in Central and East Gaul, it is frequently not known who actually made the bowl. While it may have been the mould-maker, the occurrence of bowls made in moulds of the same style but in different fabrics and with different bowl-finishers' stamps show there was a trade in moulds. All these factors serve to confuse analysis of bowls made in moulds of a single decorative style.

The mould clearly had to be made in the shape of the required form. The forms' shapes were partly dictated by the need to be able to remove the vessel from the mould. This is why the Déchelette 67 form is only decorated on the lower zone. Moulds were made of clay, or at least those which have survived were. Plaster is the only realistic alternative, usually used for lamps or terracottas but unknown for samian. Before the vessels dried and were fired the decoration had to be laid out by being impressed into the mould wall.

Decorative schemes

First the framework of decoration was decided. There were four main types: free-style, winding scrolls, horizontal zones and panels. All require an upper and lower boundary. For the first two types this was all that was necessary. Free-style (usually an aimless animal chase) and winding scrolls (usually endless vegetation) require a clear band around the bowl (figures 6 and 7). Zonal decoration required additional horizontal boundaries to create parallel zones with separate schemes of decoration (figure 8). Panel decoration is more complex and used vertical boundaries with horizontal boundaries to create combinations of panels, square and rectangular, repeated usually four times around the circumference of the mould (figure 9).

6. Free-style. All Central Gaulish Dr 37 bowls. Upper left: Paternus II style *c.*160-90. Lower left: Attianus style *c.*125-50. Right: Quintilianus Group style *c.*125-50 (this sherd also uses zones, see figure 8).

7. Winding scrolls. All are Dr 37 bowls. Upper left: Central Gaulish *c.*160-90. Upper right, lower left, and centre bottom: Central Gaulish Cinnamus style *c.*145-80. Lower right: East Gaulish, Belsus II style, late second, early third century.

8. Zonal designs. Upper left: South Gaulish Dr 29, upper zone and rim *c*.55-70. Upper right: South Gaulish Dr 37 *c*.70-85. Lower left: South Gaulish Dr 37 *c*.70-85. Lower right: Central Gaulish Dr 37, X-9 style *c*.100-30.

9. Panel designs. Upper left: South Gaulish Dr 37 *c*.70-100. Lower left: Central Gaulish Dr 37 Drusus I style *c*.100-25. Upper right: Central Gaulish Dr 37, Deoccus style *c*.165-200. Lower right: East Gaulish Dr 37, Cobnertus I style, late second, early third century.

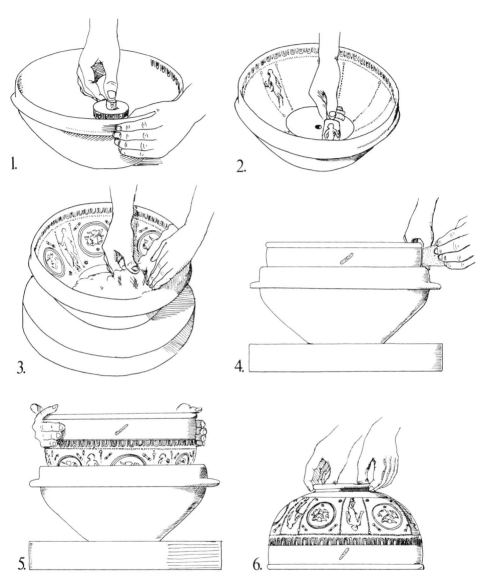

10. Manufacture of mould-decorated samian. 1. With the mould still soft the ovolos are impressed with a rotary tool. 2. Next the decorative borders are laid out and poinçons used to impress the individual motifs. 3. Once the mould has been fired it can be transferred to the wheel and clay pressed into the mould as it turns. 4. The bowl is drawn up above the mould and has its rim shaped and finished with a template. It might receive a bowl-finisher's stamp as here. 5. Once the bowl has dried and shrunk it can be withdrawn from the mould, helped by a hole in the mould's base. 6. With the bowl out and trimmed the base can be affixed. The bowl is then ready to be dipped in slip and itself fired in a stack with others.

11. Mould-makers' guidelines. On both these Central Gaulish sherds of early second-century date the guidelines used by the mould-maker to lay out the decoration have left impressions on the bowl. Left: The line for the basal wreath is visible (by Drusus I). Right: A vertical line crosses the basal wreath to guide the panel divisions above (X-10 style).

Above the top boundary was usually a row of ovolos, a series of egg-shaped ornaments separated by tongues with an innumerable variety of terminals (figure 10, *1*). The Dr 29 form, a bowl form almost entirely confined to the South Gaulish industry up to *c*.85, never has ovolos. The boundaries were first marked out with guidelines (figure 11) and then made up with round bead-rows, square bead-rows, wavy lines or, less commonly, astragali (small) cigar-shaped details with collars and buds at either end) (figure 10, *2*). Straight lines are rare, although the impressions of guidelines are sometimes visible on the bowls (figure 11). The boundaries often follow irregular paths and are frequently smudged, showing how samian was just as subject to poor workmanship as any modern industry. Sometimes the panels were not carefully measured out and odd extra ones had to be inserted to fill up the space.

Poinçons (decorative details)

Poinçons were decorative details made in raised relief and with handles to be used as punches (figure 12). They were pushed into the mould to leave an impression (figure 10, *2*). Some figures or leaves are of standard types used by many mould-makers and are so similar that they indicate the existence of a separate poinçon industry. Even so, the minor variations in standard types can help identify a mould-maker's work. Almost all mould-makers used their own special poinçons somewhere on the mould in the Central Gaulish industry, whereas in South Gaul fewer work-

12. Poinçons. These poinçons may have come from the site of the Central Gaulish potter Libertus' workshop although there is now some doubt about their authenticity. Nevertheless they still show what one of these tools for impressing decoration into the mould must have looked like. The figure is 5 cm high. (Copyright: British Museum.)

shops can be distinguished in this way. Some of the actual poinçons used have survived. Sometimes a mould-maker might use an old bowl made by someone else to copy poinçons. This might be done by taking an impression of a figure off a bowl and then using this as a mould in which to cast the copied poinçons. These show themselves by being identical to older types but smaller because samian clay shrinks significantly during the manufacturing process as it has very little filler. Alternatively, the older bowl was simply used as a model.

Decoration

Within the framework the motifs that made up the decoration were inserted next. Below the lower boundary might be a wreath of leaves of some sort. Between the boundaries the action was laid out, involving a seemingly infinite variety of animals, men, gods, women, goddesses, plants and other inanimate objects. Some clearly belong to mainstream classical mythology and the Roman pantheon. Others may recall half-forgotten Gallo-Celtic mythology in romanised form or portray everyday scenes such as gladiatorial combats. The range of quality is extensive. Some scenes are vivid and beautifully executed, others are clumsy and unappealing.

Bowl-finishers

Once the mould was fired the bowl could be made. Evidence from excavations of East Gaulish samian potteries suggests that the mould was rotated on a wheel while the samian clay was pressed into the mould (figure 10, *3*). The rim was drawn up above the mould and rounded off, probably with templates (figure 10, *4*). At this stage the person who had actually made the bowl might place his name-stamp in the rim area, or within the bowl on the bottom. Samian clay is very fine and has very little filler. In contrast, coarse wares contain much filler, usually sand, grit, ground potsherds (grog) or shells. Lack of filler makes the finished vessel less resistant to heat in normal usage and weak whilst still wet, although the mould provided support. However, it also means that the clay shrinks considerably on drying, an essential requirement if the vessel was to be withdrawn from the mould to be fired (figure 10, *5*). It was also essential for producing sharp detail on the bowl. At this stage much of the smudging sometimes so evident on the finished product occurred. Once the bowl was removed, the footstand could be luted on (glued to the bowl with liquid clay) (figure 10, *6*). However, the bases on Dr 29 bowls may have been cut from the bottom of the moulded pot, unlike the attached bases of Dr 30s and 37s. Samian bowls were coated with slip by dipping them straight into it. They were held around the base as this was done and sometimes conspicuous fingerprints were left on the bowl (figure 28, *2*).

Firing techniques

Once coated with slip and dried, the vessel could be stacked with others and placed in the kiln for firing. Some bowls were kept separate with clay rings; more usually the grit picked up by the bases of bowls while drying served to separate them in the kiln. This often left a gritty impression inside the bowl below. In use this wore off but survives on bowls broken while still fairly new.

The most accessible modern record of a samian kiln is that of the excavations carried out by M. R. Hull at Colchester. Name-stamp evidence on the site shows that it was almost certainly established by potters who had emigrated from East Gaul somewhere around 160. The kiln was about 2.5 metres

(8 feet) wide and had a 5 metre (16 foot) long flue which ran right under the circular-shaped kiln proper. The wreckage of the kiln as discovered was associated with a number of clay pipes or tubes which may have been designed to carry the heat through the kiln but prevented the fumes from damaging the bowls' gloss finish. The process used is known as oxidisation; that is, the supply of oxygen was not restricted. This allows the red colour to develop. Reduction is the opposite process and produces a black finish. Some potters did manufacture black samian, most notably the Hadrianic potter Libertus, who worked in Central Gaul.

Modern experiments on firing samian-style pottery have shown that a temperature of around 1000 C (2200 F) was needed to produce the required red colour. What is not so clear is how many bowls might be produced in each kiln firing. Graffiti from South Gaulish kilns show that plain vessels could be fired in single loads of 20-30,000. Allowing for the vessels to be stacked inside one another, the Colchester kiln's approximate volume of around 7.5 cubic metres (80 cubic feet) would have accommodated about 2500-3000 Dr 37s, depending on their size. It is even less clear how frequent firings were, so calculations of total output are almost impossible to make.

Samian shipments

Numbers must have been huge as Roman merchant ships had a capacity of, at most, about 100 tonnes (98 tons). If 10 per cent was a cargo of samian then about 6500 Dr 37s weighing at most 1.5 kg (3 pounds 5 ounces) each could have been carried, or 20,000 Dr 31s at 0.5 kg (1 pound 2 ounces), in a single shipment. Archaeologists have at their disposal a tiny proportion of what might have been imported to Britain, let alone other provinces. But the proportions are purely speculative and we have no idea of how frequently samian cargoes arrived in Britain.

3
South Gaul

Background

Principal centres. La Graufesenque, Montans, Banassac (figure 2).

Fabric. Claudian (41-54) products have a pink-orange fabric but more important is the hard glossy slip. Neronian (54-68) products are not as brightly coloured but the slip may be more brilliant. Flavian (69-100) vessels have a pink fabric with obvious cream or white flecks with a red slip that is noticeably less smooth than earlier products.

Principal potters. M. Crestio, Crucuro, Frontinus, Germanus, Iustus, Mommo, Mercator, Severus, Vitalis, Cosius Rufinus.

Distribution. South Gaulish samian was extensively distributed across Gaul, Spain, North Africa and Britain. In some respects this reflects the lack of local competition such as African red slip ware, which did not appear until the second century. The route to Britain may have involved a river trip down the Garonne to the Bay of Biscay and then on by sea but perhaps more likely was an overland route to Narbonne and then a voyage right round the Iberian peninsula to Britain.

South Gaul was the main source of all samian for Roman Britain from the invasion of 43 until about 110. Late Montans products continued to arrive well into the second century but the quantity was minimal and the quality poor. The source of the vast majority was La Graufesenque.

Potters. Although a number of major South Gaulish workshops can be identified from name-stamps it has proved difficult to discuss the decorated work in terms of styles. Unlike Central and East Gaul, South Gaulish poinçons seem to have been used by many mould-makers. Moulds seem to have been sold widely amongst La Graufesenque's bowl-finishers. The situation is worsened for the specialist by the fact that very few mould-makers or bowl-finishers ever stamped their work. Nevertheless it seems increasingly clear that poinçon-, mould- and bowl-makers may have operated in small groups or 'families'. In time it may be possible to draw up accurate tables or schemes of who supplied whom and associate these with styles. In the meantime South Gaulish decorated samian has usually to be discussed in terms of parallels for the motifs found on signed bowls or bowls occurring in closely dated contexts. This can be more accurate

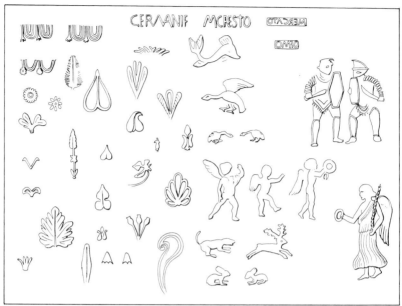

13. South Gaulish decorative details. This shows some of the more popular South Gaulish types and makers' stamps. There were thousands of poinçons used but many are variations on these basic types. All to a scale of about 1:2. (After Knorr.)

than for some second-century Gaulish material (figure 13).

The South Gaulish factories produced all the main forms of bowls carrying moulded decoration. Until the late 70s the commonest form was the carinated Dr 29 (figures 14 and 18) although during the period the profile became increasingly angular (a carination is an angle caused by a sudden change in direction in the profile of a pot). At around 85 the Dr 37 hemispherical bowl (figure 15), first introduced c.70, replaced it permanently. The only obvious decorative differences are the absence of the ovolo on the Dr 29 and the two zones, dictated by its carinated profile. The other forms are always less common (figures 16 and 17).

Claudian-Neronian period (c.43-68)

Samian found in Britain is most likely to be post-43. A useful British group of this material is the Colchester 'shop' burned down in the Boudican rebellion in 60, which contained a stock of samian. Samian of this date usually occurs in Britain only on sites closely associated with the early stages of the Roman conquest,

14. South Gaulish Dr 29 bowl stamped by the bowl-finisher Celadus *c.*55-70. (Copyright: British Museum.)

15. South Gaulish Dr 37 in the style of the potter Mommo *c.*70-85. (Copyright: British Museum.)

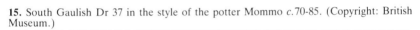

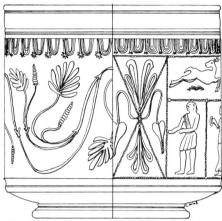

16. South Gaulish Dr 30. Composite drawing showing on the left a design of *c.*40-55 with an elegant winding scroll and on the right a panel design more typical of the second half of the first century. To a scale of about 1:2.

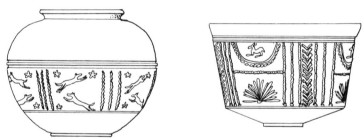

17. South Gaulish Déchelette 67 jar (left) and Knorr 78 bowl (right). Produced mainly in the period *c.*70-100. To a scale of about 1:3.

18. South Gaulish Dr 29. The standard decorated form until *c.*85. On the left is a Claudian-style bowl with curved profile and winding scrolls in both zones, separated by a band of chevrons. On the right is the more angular Flavian variety, showing use of panels and more figure-types. To a scale of about 1:2.

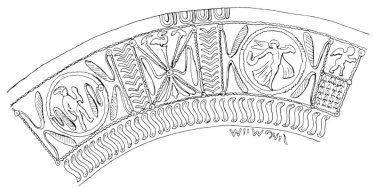

19. South Gaulish Dr 37 made in a mould signed by the mould-maker Memor. This bowl was amongst 90 unused Dr 29s and 37s found in a crate along with 37 oil lamps in a house in Pompeii. Clearly they cannot have been made after the date of Vesuvius' eruption in August 79. To a scale of about 1:3. (After Atkinson.)

20. South Gaulish Dr 37. Introduced *c.*70 and after *c.*85 the standard decorated samian bowl. On the left the connection with the Flavian Dr 29 is obvious. The zones remain with their panels — early Flavian. On the right a later Flavian variety with panels spread across the decoration. To a scale of about 1:2.

such as forts and the towns of London, St Albans and Colchester. A widespread romanised civilian market had yet to be created. Chief decorative characteristics are winding scrolls or wreaths in both zones of the Dr 29, with innumerable variations in detail such as the leaf terminal. Sometimes small birds were placed about the scroll. In the Neronian period medallions became incorporated into the scrolls, sometimes containing animal types such as dolphins. Usually the quality of moulding at this time was very high, producing elegant and attractive decoration (figures 14 and 18).

Flavian period (c.69-100/110)

The most important group of samian of this period is the unpacked crate of South Gaulish samian found in Pompeii, and thus not post-dating 79, giving important evidence for the styles of the period and the dates of activity for the potters whose work is represented, such as Mommo (figure 15) and Memor (figure 19). In Britain a useful, but very small, group is the samian found at the legionary fortress of Inchtuthil which was occupied only for the years *c*.84-7. This was a period when samian flooded into Britain as a result of the Flavian reconstruction after the Boudican revolt. Despite the insecurity in the north, towns like London began boom periods of commercial growth.

The more angular Dr 29 of the period was accompanied by the insertion of panels into the decorated zones, usually with alternating motifs such as a pair of hounds, then a panel of chevrons (a V-shaped motif), followed by a panel containing hares, and so on. The lower zone was as likely to contain a more elaborate winding scroll and was separated from the upper zone by a cordon, frequently emphasised with a continuous wreath (figure 18). Figure-types are generally much more common and this was especially true of the Dr 37s, which might be decorated with zones or panels and occasionally free-style. However, there is a considerable contrast with the lifelike figures of Trajanic Central Gaul. South Gaulish figures are usually presented in stiff postures with rather unrealistic looking limbs and rarely with satisfactory small detail. Dogs, hares and small birds abound but there is also a wide range of robot-like gladiator pairs, victories and cupids with absurdly fat legs. These are in marked contrast to the inanimate motifs which were still produced competently even late in South Gaul's period of activity. Common space-fillers are a large variety of chevrons, lozenges, arrowheads and gadroons (similar to long thin round-ended petals) (figure 20).

Decline

There was a conspicuous deterioration in the quality of South Gaulish decorated samian towards the end of the first century AD. The characteristic wavy-line borders become smudged and irregular. The quality of moulding declines and the slip shows a tendency to flake off around details. The reasons for this are unknown. Perhaps the products were outdated in terms of style or they may have been too expensive. There is, however, no certain evidence that the potters emigrated to Central Gaul.

4
Central Gaul

Background

By about the beginning of the second century the South Gaulish industry was in a sufficient state of decline for new samian industries elsewhere to fill the gap. The most successful centres were in Central Gaul, which already had a tradition of local pottery-making. Les Martres-de-Veyre dominated samian output until c.125; then Lezoux took over until the end of the second century, when its industry abruptly collapsed, also for unknown reasons (figure 2).

Samian had been manufactured at Lezoux during the first century AD. Although a serviceable product, not very much was exported, no doubt reflecting the strength of the South Gaulish industry. The fabric tends to be micaceous and the slip is prone to flaking off in time. The latter feature marks it out as a site-find though this would hardly have been relevant to the original purchaser.

South Gaulish connections

Not surprisingly the Central Gaulish potters borrowed much from South Gaul. This included the basic bowl forms of Dr 37 and 30; even the abandoned Dr 29 form was occasionally produced. Decorative features are essentially similar. The ovolo is almost always present but in increasing varieties according to workshop styles. The tightly packed wreath at the bottom of the decoration is common for most of the first half of the second century, also in increasing variety. Panel decoration remained popular but zonal decoration became less usual. The elaborate winding scrolls and free-style scenes owed much to South Gaulish potters.

The workshops of Central Gaul are, however, far better understood than those of South Gaul. The styles are more distinct and individual and in many cases can be confidently attributed to known workshops. This is because styles are fairly consistent and name-stamps relatively common. Some who did not stamp or sign their products have distinctive and recognisable styles and are generally referred to as, for example, 'X-1' or 'X-2'.

Trajanic potters at Les Martres-de-Veyre (c.100-25)

Fabric. A distinctive smooth pink-orange fabric; the slip is generally a lustrous waxy orange.

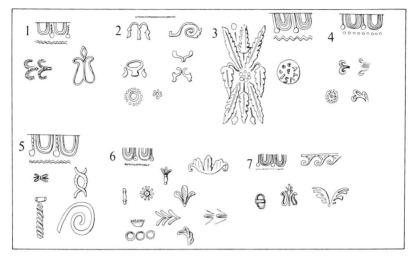

21. Central Gaulish Trajanic decorative details. This shows some of the most frequently used decorative details; some were used by more than one style. 1. X-2. 2. X-3 (Drusus I) who also uses X-2's ovolo. 3. X-4 (Igocatus). 4. 'Potter of the Rosette'. 5. Medetus-Ranto. 6. X-11/12 (Ioenalis). 7. X-13/14 (Donnaucus). To a scale of about 1:2. (After Stanfield.)

Principal potters. X-1, X-2, Drusus I (X-3), Igocatus (X-4), 'Potter of the Rosette', Medetus, Ranto, Ioenalis and Donnaucus.

The small group of workshops here rarely identify themselves although their styles mark out their separate identities. Most of their work was produced at Les Martres-de-Veyre but some was certainly made at Lezoux as well. The most important mould-manufacturer is known as Drusus I. Until a bowl bearing his mould-signature was found he was known as the 'Anchor Potter' or X-3. His style is conspicuously original (figures 21, *2* and cover). A number of the decorative motifs he used are unique to him, especially his spiral. He frequently experimented with replacing the ovolo by another of his motifs, such as the anchor or the little pair of dolphins. His work tends to be made up of small panels, each crammed with his motifs. A favourite subject was a pair of opposed gladiators. Drusus used some of the same motifs as another mould-maker called Igocatus (known as X-4 before a stamped bowl was found) and an anonymous style called X-2 (figure 21, *1,3).* It is possible that they worked closely together, perhaps trading poinçons.

Other important potters of the period are mostly anonymous, for example the 'Potter of the Rosette' (figure 21, *4)*. A number of bowl-finishers of the period are known: Medetus, Ranto, Tasgillus, Ioenalis and Donnaucus. They are a particularly confusing group because they are associated with bowls in a number of anonymous decorative styles by potters known as X-8, X-9, X-10 (for Medetus, Ranto and Tasgillus), X-11, X-12, X-13 and X-14 (for Ioenalis and Donnaucus) (figure 21, *5-7)*.

Were all these potters workers in one operation or were they independent craftsmen? They worked together closely enough to share kiln loads, as piles of fused wasters found at the kiln sites show (figure 22). Rates of output differed; for example, Drusus I's bowls are far more common than X-2's, which suggests some autonomy.

22. A stack of fused wasters, probably found at Les Martres-de-Veyre in Central Gaul, of early second-century date. A number of bowls in several different styles of the Trajanic period have been over-fired and melted together. This shows that the bowl-finishers were sharing kilns or that one bowl-finisher had bought his moulds from a number of the Trajanic mould-makers. (Copyright: British Museum.)

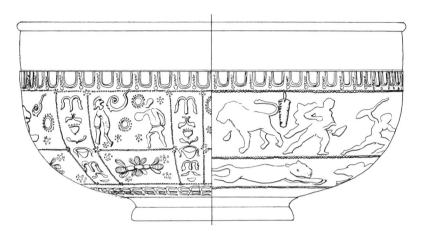

23. Central Gaulish Dr 37. On the left is a Trajanic bowl in the style known as Drusus I or X-3. Panels and basal wreaths are crammed with original motifs centred on a gladiator fight. On the right a Hadrianic bowl in the style of Sissus I of the Quintilianus Group shows the typical retention of basal wreath and wavy lines with free-style activity retained in zones reminiscent of South Gaul; the Trajanic clutter has diminished. To a scale of about 1:2.

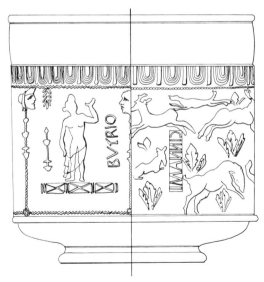

24. Central Gaulish Dr 30. On the left a design in the style of the Hadrianic potter Butrio and bearing his advertisement stamp. On the right a free-style scene by the dominant Antonine potter Cinnamus and also bearing his name-stamp. To a scale of about 1:2.

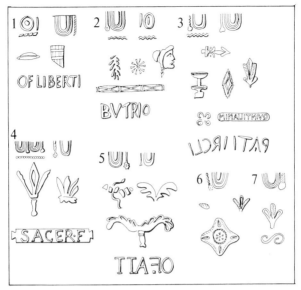

25. Central Gaulish Hadrianic decorative details. This shows some of the details used by the major workshops of this period and their name-stamps. 1. Libertus. 2. Butrio. 3. Quintilianus Group. 4. Sacer. 5. Attianus. 6. X-5. 7. X-6. To a scale of about 1:2. (After Stanfield.)

The Trajanic potters are notable for their exuberant styles, though this sometimes results in energetically cluttered scenes. Characteristic features are delicacy of motifs and neatly executed borders (figure 23). The Trajanic potters seem to have produced far less material than their South Gaulish predecessors; there were far fewer of them and they may have been in operation for only a very short time during the period to which their work has been assigned. This may mean that a single Trajanic sherd is of equal dating significance to several sherds of the previous period.

Hadrianic potters at Lezoux (c.125-45)

Fabric. A pale brown-orange with visible mica; the slip is also orange but is less smooth and lustrous than at Les Martres-de-Veyre.

Principal potters. Libertus, Butrio, the Quintilianus Group, the Sacer-Attianus Group, the anonymous potters X-5 and X-6, Medetus and Ranto at Lezoux (see 'Trajanic potters', above).

26. Central Gaulish Dr 37. On the left an Antonine-style winding scroll and figures. The decoration is noticeably heavier, bead-rows are used for borders and the basal wreath has vanished. On the right an Antonine panel design in the style of the potter Doeccus showing many of his favourite motifs. To a scale of about 1:2.

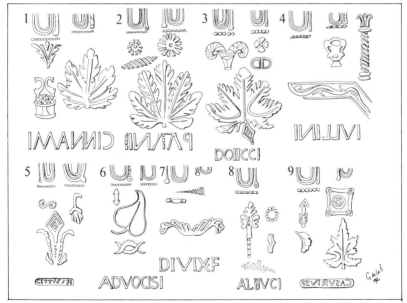

27. Central Gaulish Antonine decorative details. This shows some of the favourite motifs used by the major workshops and their name-stamps. 1. Cinnamus. 2. Paternus II. 3. Doeccus. 4. Iullinus. 5. Cettus ('Small "S" Potter'). 6. Advocisus. 7. Divixtus. 8. Albucius. 9. Casurius. To a scale of about 1:2. (After Stanfield.)

In the Hadrianic period and later the workshops of Central Gaul generally cease to be anonymous. Names are common enough in the decoration for the distinctive styles of the period to be attached to those names. From a stylistic point of view there is a tendency to increase the amount of empty space in the field of decoration, which contrasts with the elegant congestion of Trajanic times. Basal wreaths and ridges (at the bottom of the decoration) and wavy-line borders are typical Hadrianic features (figures 23 and 24).

The products of the Libertus workshop are not very common but he is important because many of the later Lezoux figure-types, perhaps a quarter, were originally introduced by him (figure 25, *1*). He made black samian (see chapter 2) and a number of unusual bowl types (figure 5). Butrio made vessels in a similar style and may have worked with Libertus (figure 25, *2*). Their vessels are dominated by free-style scenes featuring a large number of human or divine figure-types (figure 24).

The Quintilianus Group seems to have included a number of potters such as Ianuarius I, Paterclus and Sissus I, who made moulds broadly in the Quintilianus house-style, though each with a degree of originality. The latter three tend to place hand-written signatures below the decoration, suggesting their sub-ordinate status. Basal wreaths and panels separated by wavy lines abound, filled with a number of figure-types, small rosettes and leaves. The quality of the slip was unusually good (figure 25, *3*).

The Sacer-Attianus Group may have been more of a partnership. The two potters shared many motifs and it is sometimes difficult to attribute sherds to one or the other (figure 25, *4-5*).

Two of the anonymous potters whose styles date to this period are known as X-5 and X-6. Their products are not infrequently found but their workshops may have been small enough to make signing moulds and bowls unnecessary. Their styles show the usual Hadrianic features but they also had their own motifs which distinguish them from other Hadrianic potters (figure 25, *6-7*).

Antonine potters at Lezoux (c.145-200)

Fabric. As for Hadrianic potters but with an increasing tendency to rough finishes caused by coarser clay being used for moulds.

Principal potters. Cinnamus, Paternus II, Doeccus, Cettus ('Small "S" Potter'), Advocisus, Divixtus, Albucius, Iullinus and Casurius.

28. Dr 37 bowl made in a mould stamped by Cinnamus of Central Gaul. Found shattered in fragments by a Kent Archaeological Society excavation beneath a roof-fall on the site of a villa at Sedgebrook, near Plaxtol in Kent, in 1986. 1 (above). The design shows medallions containing a figure incorporated into a winding scroll. 2 (below). The view of the base shows the fingerprints and smudges caused when the bowl was dipped into the slip in the pottery workshop. *c.*155-75; diameter 26.5 cm, height 14.5 cm, weight *c.*1.5 kg when complete. (Courtesy of the Fairlawne Estate.)

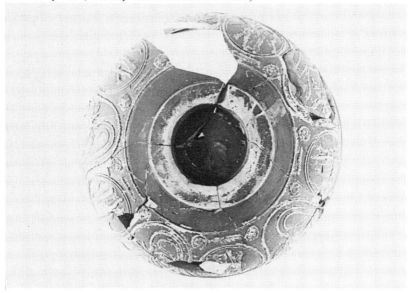

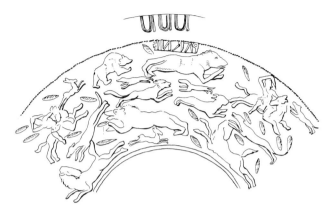

29. Dr 37 bowl made in a mould stamped by Paternus II of Central Gaul *c.*160-90. The design shows an energetic free-style animal chase. To a scale of about 1:3. (After Stanfield.)

In this period there was a marked decline in the general aesthetic quality of Central Gaulish products though the bowls themselves were still well made. They tend to be larger and heavier than earlier products but the requirements of mass production seem to have encouraged the use of fewer poinçons per mould and the use of old moulds, resulting in bowls with less inspired, worn decoration. The basal wreaths virtually disappear. Borders are almost always made up of bead-rows, rather than wavy lines. The period was dominated by the styles of a few major workshops which probably sold their moulds widely. Some advertised themselves with large stamps placed in the decoration (figures 26 and 27).

The workshop of Cinnamus (*c.*145-80) was the most important source of Antonine decorated samian. On the Antonine Wall, which helps date his period of activity, two-thirds of the decorated samian can be attributed to this workshop. Some bowl-finishers (such as Tittius and Cintusmus) are known to have used moulds made by Cinnamus. Also, bowls appear in different fabrics, suggesting that either Cinnamus operated several work-shops or that his moulds were sold quite widely. He also appears to have had mould-makers such as Cerealis who worked with or for him, manufacturing moulds in the house-style, which tends to be repetitive within any one design itself, although Cinnamus' range of motifs was very extensive. Some originated in Trajanic times. Particularly common for Cinnamus are bowls with winding scrolls featuring large leaves interspersed with medallions containing a figure-type, or panel decoration divided up by large bead-rows (figures 24, 27, *1* and 28).

The work of the potter Paternus II (*c.*160-90) is similar in style to that of Cinnamus but most of the motifs are different. A large advertisement stamp within the decoration was also used. The most interesting feature of his work is that, although his period of activity overlaps with that of Cinnamus, practically no Paternus II material turns up on the Antonine Wall. This has helped to date his material because presumably Paternus II was not active until this frontier had been abandoned (figures 27, *2* and 29).

Doeccus (*c.*160-200) operated over a similar time-span but produced higher-quality material distinguished by his extremely well moulded motifs. He favoured panel decoration filled with a large range of leaves and figure-types (figures 27, *3* and 26).

30. Dr 30 bowl made by Divixtus of Lezoux *c.*145-70. (Copyright: British Museum.)

31. Dr 37 bowl made by Casurius of Lezoux *c.*165-200. (Copyright: British Museum.)

Other important potters of the period were: Iullinus (*c.*160-200) (figure 27, *4*); Cettus ('Small "S" Potter') (*c.*135-65) (figure 27, *5*); Advocisus (*c.*150-80) (figure 27, *6*); Divixtus (*c.*145-70) (figures 27, *7* and 30); Albucius (*c.*150-80) (figure 27, *8*); Casurius (*c.*165-200) (figures 27, *9* and 31).

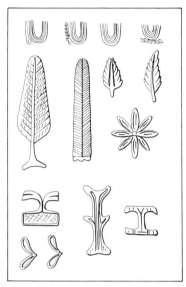

32. East Gaulish decorative details. Many East Gaulish details were copied from Central Gaulish designs. These examples show a few which do not occur on Central Gaulish designs and give a flavour of some Rheinzabern motifs which were locally produced. To a scale of about 1:2.

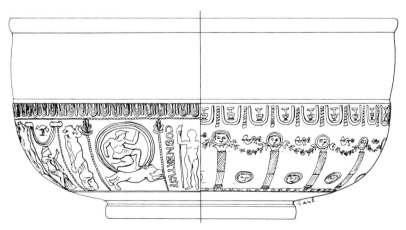

33. East Gaulish Dr 37. On the left is a design in the style of the Rheinzabern potter Cobnertus III and bearing his name-stamp. The connection with the Antonine Central Gaulish potters is obvious. On the right is a design in the style of Dexter of Trier showing an original design with his vase ovolo but a rather repetitive use of the same poinçon. Both styles *c.*150-90. To a scale of about 1:2.

5
East Gaul

Background

Main centres. Rheinzabern, Trier, Chémery, La Madeleine, Blickweiler, Heiligenberg and Lavoye (Argonne) (figure 2).

The name East Gaul is misleading because there was no homogeneity of style or fabric to justify such a collective title. East Gaul is merely a convenient geographical term used to refer to a number of samian-producing centres most active in the second to early third centuries.

Origins. The East Gaulish samian industries were dominated by Rheinzabern and Trier. Some potters had certainly left Central Gaul: for example, the Hadrianic potter Austrus left Lezoux and started work in Blickweiler. The most consistent feature of East Gaulish decorated samian was its stylistic debt to Central Gaul. As has been seen above, this derivative tendency is common to all samian manufacture. In some cases whole moulds seem to have been brought from Central to East Gaul, only the fabric revealing the bowl's source. Rheinzabern and Trier bowls are particularly characterised by their high rims, thick walls, heavy bases and uneven slip.

Distribution. East Gaulish products are principally dispersed in the provinces of origin although the general area produced a number of specialist wares which came to Britain right up to the fourth century. Most of the East Gaulish samian which does occur in Britain is at sites on or near the east coast, though this is by no means exclusive. In London generally only around 4 per cent of the decorated samian is from East Gaul; most of that is from Rheinzabern. Later East Gaulish samian tends to be less closely dated than other samian because there are few published instances of comprehensive groups being recovered from levels associated with historically dated events. However, the New Fresh Wharf site in London produced a large and very important group of East Gaulish samian. This and the study of name-stamps means that the material has yet to fulfil its potential.

Rheinzabern (c.140-260)

Fabric. Usually orange, lacking Lezoux's mica; later wares are associated with a patchy orange-brown matt slip.

Principal potters. Belsus, B. F. Atto, Peregrinus, Cerealis, Cobnertus, Comitialis, Primitivus, Perpetuus, Iulius, Reginus,

Respectinus.

Rheinzabern products usually date to the Antonine period and later, bearing most resemblance to Antonine products of Central Gaul. A number of potters who worked here are testified at other East Gaulish centres, particularly Heiligenberg. Moving around seems to have been quite common amongst East Gaulish potters, which adds to the difficulty of understanding the industry. One potter called Domitianus seems to have worked at Heiligenberg, Kraherwald, Waiblingen and Rheinzabern.

The most conspicuous features of Rheinzabern decorated samian, though these do not always occur, are a lack of border beneath the ovolos and some ovolos which are not separated from one another by tongues (figure 32). Otherwise the general layouts of free-style, panel and winding scrolls are very similar to Central Gaulish designs although motifs are spaced further apart. A number of figure-types are even exactly the same. However, there is a conspicuous heaviness of moulding (figure 33).

There seems to have been little local capacity to manufacture poinçons because from the later second century the quantity available simply declines. Bowls tend to feature fewer motifs repeated more often. Presumably, as poinçons broke or became damaged, they were discarded and could not be replaced. The long-term consequence of this was that mould-makers resorted to decorating a mould with a single poinçon or even simply scratching designs. Thereafter incised, rouletted or barbotine decoration, already well established, became the norm (see chapter 7). However, very few of these occur in Britain because by the mid third century the Oxfordshire, New Forest and Nene Valley potteries were satisfying Romano-British demand for fine wares and produced a number of imitation samian types as part of their extensive repertoire.

For the most part the Rheinzabern potteries operated in a manner similar to those of Central Gaul. Bowls carried the impression of name-stamps placed in the moulds, making it possible to attribute decorative motifs to certain workshops (figure 33).

Trier (c.125-260 in Britain, elsewhere in north-west Europe probably somewhat later)

Fabric. Earlier products are similar to Lezoux's but instead of the mica dense white inclusions occur; slip has a brownish tone. Late products have a yellow-brown or pinkish fabric containing small particles of quartz which sometimes jump from the surface

34. A Dr 37 bowl made in Trier and said to have been found in the sea off Kent. Late second, early third century. (Copyright: British Museum.)

in the kiln leaving tiny pits. The slip started off as a matt orange-red but degenerated towards brown and tended to flake off.

Principal potters. Dexter, Censor, Werkstatt ('workshop' = anonymous) styles I and II, Criciro, Dubitus-Dubitatus, Afer and the Primanus Group.

Although potters like Dexter and Censor attempted to recover some of the quality of much earlier samian, and their products can be very well made and attractively designed, the industry of Trier declined as did the rest of East Gaul. Dexter, for example, used an ovolo with a vase in place of the central tongue (figure 33). However, unlike Rheinzabern potters, those at Trier carried on making new poinçons but in increasingly barbarous style. In some cases there seems to be evidence for third-century Trier potters re-using old moulds.

35. A fragment of mould (26 cm wide) and a sherd (8 cm high) from a Dr 37 bowl. Both from the samian kiln site at Colchester. (Courtesy of the Colchester and Essex Museum, and on display in the British Museum.)

6
Romano-British samian

Colchester samian

Around 160 a group of potters, numbering between fourteen and twenty, became engaged in the production of samian at Colchester. Some were certainly immigrants from East Gaul, such as Minuso who had previously worked at Trier, amongst other places. The samian kiln itself bears much resemblance to types known in East Gaul. At least two decorative styles have been recognised at Colchester but they are anonymous because neither potter stamped the moulds or the finished bowls. Fragments of more than 400 moulds were recovered. Nevertheless, while many of the poinçons seem to have been locally made the overall style of the Colchester moulds and bowls resemble East Gaulish products, reflecting the potters' backgrounds. Their products seem barely to have been traded beyond Colchester itself although it is possible that minor fragments of their work have passed unnoticed in some excavated groups further afield.

The failure of the Colchester decorated samian manufacturers to capture even a small piece of the Romano-British decorated samian market is the most significant feature of the industry. The Colchester samian is mostly acceptably designed and the kiln was a large one. Being made in Britain, the pottery should have been cheaper and it was made near the coast where it could easily have been shipped north to Hadrian's Wall or south to London. A demand must have been anticipated and the East Gaulish potters presumably moved to Colchester because they expected to gain an advantage from doing so. One can only conclude that the Romano-British market liked the Central Gaulish material more and that those who traded the Central Gaulish material had an organised and efficient distribution system coupled with competitive pricing. Certainly the Colchester clay was of inferior quality. The excavator of the Colchester site believed that the Colchester samian was manufactured for only a short time. An abrupt termination of activity might be suggested by the discovery of some moulds which had yet to be fired (figure 35).

The 'Aldgate-Pulborough Potter'

The fifteen or so surviving examples of the work of this potter are amongst the most enigmatic of all samian products. On the one hand his bowls were so substandard that it is difficult to

36. A large sherd from a Dr 37 bowl, probably a waster, by the 'Aldgate-Pulborough' potter; a free-style 'hunt' scene is in progress. Found at Aldgate in London. (Copyright: British Museum.)

believe that they were saleable. On the other, fragments have turned up in Bristol, London, Silchester, Chichester and Pulborough/Wigginholt, West Sussex, showing that they were not only marketable but were fairly widespread despite a small output. Evidence for manufacture has been found in the form of a waster at Aldgate in London and moulds at a villa in Pulborough. This suggests that the potter may have travelled about, establishing temporary kilns in suitable locations. His work used a number of poinçons which can be associated with a handful of Central Gaulish potters who operated from *c*.125-50. However, they are all slightly smaller, suggesting that he used sherds from original Central Gaulish bowls. His trademarks, apart from his motifs (which were very casually distributed about the bowl to the extent that he superimposed some) were variously to scratch and scuff the surface of the bowls leaving liberal traces of fingerprints and/or to over-fire the product causing a blistered uneven surface with flaking slip (figure 36).

Drusus I
A mould in this potter's style found in York has been interpreted as evidence of an attempt by this Central Gaulish potter (see chapter 4) to set up a 'branch' in Britain. However, the complete lack of any kiln or waster evidence makes it much more likely that the mould came to Britain in relatively recent times.

7
Other forms of decorated samian

Appliqué

This alternative type of decoration produced the most similar results to the moulded form. However, it led to a potentially far superior product and could be applied to a much wider range of vessel types, particularly jars (which could not be decorated on the upper half with moulds), for example, the Déchelette 67 (figure 5). The method involved manufacturing the decorative details separately from the vessels themselves. They were then attached to the bowl, producing an effect similar to that of modern fine wares such as Wedgwood (figure 37). It was previously practised by the Arretine potters in Italy and by potters at Pergamum in Turkey, and later on some forms of African red slip ware. However it was more time-consuming and therefore more expensive. Samian appliqué vessels are very rare apart from mortarium (mixing bowl) forms. Very occasionally Dr 37 bowls carry a few appliqué motifs amongst the moulded decoration; such a vessel was found at Fishbourne.

A number of jar types with appliqué decoration are known to have been used from about the middle of the second century. These are known as the Déchelette 72, or the 74, which is the same but has handles. A well known example from Britain is the 'Cornhill' vase, a Déchelette 72 (figure 38). This vase in particular demonstrates the relationship with other forms of Roman decorated vessels in bronze and glass because it produces relief of similar quality but it was presumably cheaper.

The Dr 45 mortarium form, made in Central and East Gaul from the late second to early third centuries, is really a plain form but its most significant feature is an appliqué lion's head luted to the upper wall (figure 39). In time the design became something more akin to a bat's head (figure 40).

Barbotine decoration

This method involves trailing semi-liquid clay across the surface of a vessel prior to dipping it in slip and was normally only used to produce a simple leaf and stalk. In practice barbotine decoration was only used on a very restricted range of vessels. The most common are the Dr 35 cup and Dr 36 bowl (figures 41 and 42). They rarely carry a potter's stamp. The barbotine decoration appears on the overhanging rim. Both forms were

37. Two sherds, probably from Déchelette 72 vases, of later second-century date, both bearing appliqué motifs.

38. The 'Cornhill' vase, a Déchelette 72 found on Cornhill in London; 27 cm high. The restoration of the rim is probably incorrect. (Copyright: British Museum.)

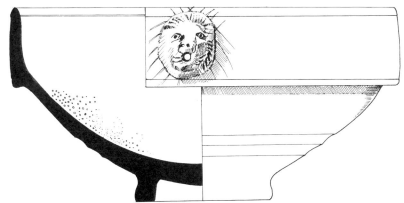

39. Dr 45 mortarium showing the appliqué lion's head. To a scale of about 1:2.

exported to Britain throughout the period of samian manufacture and can appear in all Gaulish fabrics. Some later variants have very accomplished decoration but these are unusual (figure 41). The other most likely vessel to carry this decorative style is the Curle 11 bowl, which is very similar to the Dr 35 and 36 forms but is larger, deeper and has a flange instead of a turned-over rim

40. Four examples of lions' head appliqué motifs from the Dr 45 mortarium. The lower right example bears considerable resemblance to a bat's head, in contrast to the upper left example.

(figures 41 and 42, *1*). The vessel type lasted from Flavian to Hadrianic times. Figure 43 shows a Déchelette 72 from Felixstowe with barbotine and appliqué decoration.

Rouletted decoration

With the demise of the Dr 29 in *c.*85 the practice of rouletting became more or less obsolete until the second century, when it was quite frequently used by some East Gaulish factories as an uninspired substitute for moulded decoration on some forms (figure 42, *4*). The decoration was simply achieved by rolling an appropriately patterned tool around the vessel while it was still wet.

41. Various sherds from dishes with barbotine decoration. The largest piece is from a particularly elaborate Dr 36 with a rouletted circle around the floor and is probably late second-century in date (original diameter 27 cm). On the upper left the first two smaller sherds are from more representative examples of Dr 35 and 36 cups and dishes. On the lower left are two sherds from the Curle 11 bowl, of late first-century date. A 2 pence coin is included for scale.

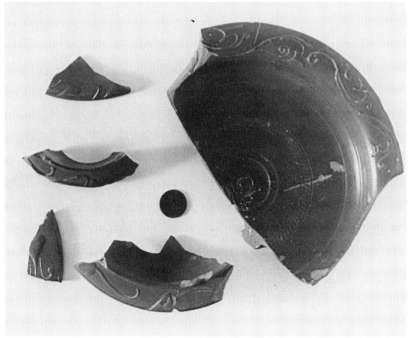

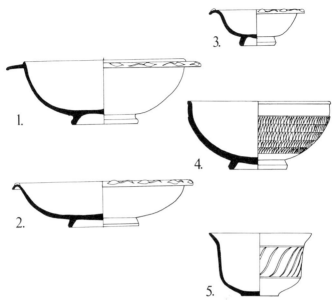

42. Samian forms with other decoration. 1. Curle 11 bowl with barbotine-decorated flange. This example is Flavian; later versions have a more curved-over flange. 2 and 3. Dr 35 cup and Dr 36 bowl with curved-over barbotine-decorated rim. Produced throughout the period. 4. Dr 37 with rouletted decoration. Mostly made in the late second-, early third-century East Gaulish factories. 5. Dr 41 with incised decoration, second century. All to a scale of about 1:4.

43. Central Gaulish Déchelette Form 72. Based on a vase from Felixstowe, this is Antonine in date and shows a combined use of appliqué work for the leaves and barbotine for the tendrils and dog. The vessel is 20.8 cm high.

Cut glass/incised decoration

Directly derived from real cut glass, this method consisted of incising the vessel and was most commonly used in East Gaul. The Déchelette 72 was usually involved but other forms include the Dr 41, which was based on glass bowl forms (figure 42, 5). In general decoration was normally in the form of curved lines, stars, buds and simple leaves.

8
Plain samian

Plain forms of samian ware are much more common as site finds than decorated forms. Despite this they usually give less information. A large number of different types of forms were made and have been classified by various specialists (figures 44 and 45). These include those who named the main decorated forms but there are others such as Ludowici, Ritterling and Curle. Some were used for a long time during the period in which samian was manufactured and survived to be copied by pottery industries which imitated samian ware. An example is the Dr 38 flanged bowl. A popular samian form introduced in the second century, it was still being copied by the Oxfordshire potteries in Britain well into the fourth century. Some forms were produced for only a few decades, such as the Dr 24 cup, which was manufactured mostly during the Claudian and Neronian periods.

Although the range of plain samian forms was so extensive, only a few occur with any great degree of regularity. It will be apparent that distinguishing sherds which are small, and lack the rim, is likely to be difficult. It is also practically impossible to estimate how many vessels are represented, whereas decorated forms can be numbered according to a minimum number of decorative schemes which can be distinguished. Minor details such as the exact form of the base are subject to considerable variation, sometimes with chronological significance. Extracting useful information from small sherds of plain samian is a skilled task. Identifying the fabric can be helpful.

Britain has produced two extremely valuable deposits of plain samian. Their value is not that they are associated with specific events but that they both involve consignments of samian which had yet to be sold to consumers. The collection of potters' stamps included gives a picture of some of the potters who were working at the same time as one another. The Wroxeter, Shropshire, group was found in the east portico of the forum and apparently involved the contents of a stall scattered during a fire which wrecked the forum after the middle of the second century (perhaps c.165-75). Curiously the stacks of samian bowls and Romano-British coarse ware mortaria were left where they had fallen and were buried during the subsequent rebuilding of the forum. Of the 197 plain samian bowls, from Central and East Gaul, 160 were of the extremely popular Dr 31 form. The bowls

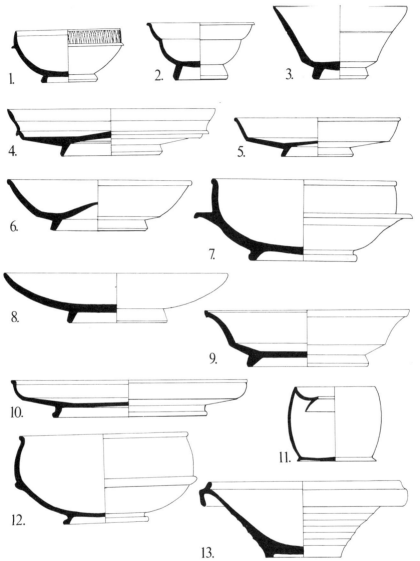

44. Plain samian forms. 1. Dr 24 cup, Claudian-Neronian. 2. Dr 27 cup, early first-century to late second. 3. Dr 33 cup, throughout the period but first-century examples usually lack the waist groove. 4. Dr 15/17 dish, mid to late first century. 5. Dr 18 dish, mid to late first century. 6. Dr 31 bowl, mid to late second century. (Dr 18/31 transitional form fills the gap.) 7. Dr 38 bowl with waist flange, later second century. 8. Dr 32 bowl, later second century, usually East Gaulish. 9. Curle 15 dish, usually second century. 10. 'Walters Form' 79 dish, later second century. 11. Ritterling 11 inkpot, made throughout the period. 12. Dr 44 bowl, similar to Dr 38 but with a waist cordon, later second century. 13. Curle 21 bowl, similar to a mortarium but without the grits, later second century. All to a scale of about 1:4.

45. Unusual plain forms. Left to right: a jug from Dymchurch, Kent (height 12.1 cm); an inkpot, Ritterling Form 11, from Colchester (height 5.5 cm); a feeding-bottle from Colchester (height 10.1 cm). (Copyright: British Museum.)

were made by a number of potters but with many duplicates. For example, Victor manufactured 37 and Elvillus 26 of them (both Central Gaulish workshops). This may suggest that some of the bowls were still in groups bought at or near the manufacturing centres.

The Pudding Pan Rock lies off the Kent coast near Whitstable.

46. A group of plain cups and dishes from the 'Pudding Pan Rock' off the coast of Kent. They probably come from the hold of a ship (or ships) wrecked in the late second century whilst bringing samian from Gaul to London. They bear encrustations typical on pottery recovered from the sea. (Copyright: British Museum.)

It was so named because of the 'pudding pans' fishermen were dredging up over two hundred years ago and selling ashore for domestic use. Antiquarian attention was drawn to this and the site has subsequently been recognised as a deposit of Antonine Central Gaulish samian (all plain) and some other goods which probably came from the· hold of a ship or ships wrecked *en route* from Gaul to London. The actual wreck or wrecks have not been located. As with Wroxeter, a number of potters' names recur, such as Cintusmus and Saturninus (figure 46). The deposit dates to probably *c.*160-200.

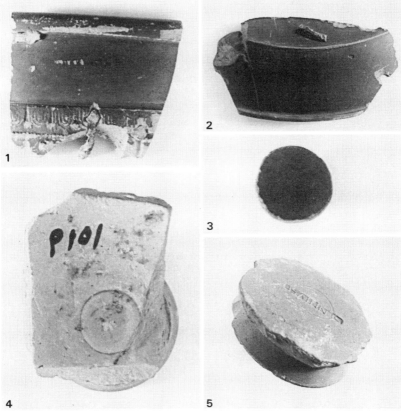

47. Various sherds of re-used samian. 1. Sherd from a Dr 37 bowl of Hadrianic date still carrying rivets which secured it to the rest of the now lost bowl. 2. Sherd from a Dr 18 bowl with part of a rivet and part of a hole drilled for another. 3. Small sherd filed down to produce a gaming counter. 4. Dr 27 cup base which has been used for grinding. 5. Dr 33 cup base which has had its wall removed and then been neatly filed down, perhaps to make it a gaming counter also, or for use as a lid.

9
Interpreting samian

Problems for the archaeologist

Samian is a brittle ware and is usually found in a very fragmentary state. This makes it difficult to assess how many vessels are represented and in some cases what type. It is important to recognise that samian was frequently re-used or repaired so the sherds may have been in use for a long time. Repaired bowls are usually decorated forms. Repairs were performed either by drilling holes and tying the sherds with metal strips or by bridging the fracture with X-shaped rivets (figure 47, *1,2*).

Vessels that have had a long life usually show some abrasion of the slip, rendering decorated sherds difficult to identify. Soil chemical conditions can hasten this and make the fabric hard to distinguish. This also raises the question of how much excavated samian is residual (see chapter 1). A samian bowl might last unbroken for a considerable period of time. It is also possible that the Roman army bought up large amounts and stored it, perhaps inadvertently pushing 'old stock' to the back of the warehouse where it might linger for years before being used.

One of the most common forms of re-use was to file down small plain sherds, sometimes a piece including the name-stamp, to make gaming counters. A similar piece drilled with a central hole might serve as a spindle whorl. The bases of broken Dr 33 cups seem to have been regarded as useful counters or lids. All the wall area was removed and the base neatly filed down (figure 47, *5)*. In some cases samian bears inscriptions known as 'graffiti' (figures 48 and 49).

Mould-decorated material can be obscure. Name-stamps within the decoration are rare. At the Billingsgate Lorry Park site, out of 589 decorated sherds only eight bear even partial stamps. The other 581 had all to be attributed to workshops on the basis of style. A significant proportion remained unidentified on stylistic grounds because they did not carry enough of the right information. For example, a sherd might carry only one identifiable motif which happened to be used by a dozen different Central Gaulish workshops from Hadrianic times up to the end of the second century.

Burnt samian can be confused with black samian. The latter was deliberately achieved by firing in reduction conditions and

48. An East Gaulish Dr 31 bowl, probably of the early third century, bearing an unusually long graffito. The word 'Victor' is visible. From Faversham, Kent. (Copyright: British Museum.)

fortunately only appears in the rarer decorated forms. Burnt samian generally goes black or a deep purple and, because of uneven intensities of fire, the discolouration may be mottled. The burning also extends across the fracture.

All of these problems conspire to limit samian's value as a site find. So how can it be of use?

Samian reports

Studies of samian, particularly decorated samian, used only to discuss the individual sherds in terms of likely source of manufacture, possibly the actual workshop, and attempt to give a date or range of dates for each piece according to the context on the site and dated parallels. Very little account was taken of what significance variations in the actual supply of samian might have had and by how much a site differed from what appears to be the norm.

It has long been recognised that the supply of Roman coins was subject to considerable variation. As a result the colossal quantities of the so-called 'barbarous radiates' have been reconsidered. These degenerate mid third-century coins are found in very large numbers and were originally thought to represent an intense period of activity on any site where they were recovered. However, it gradually became clear that the truth was that the coins were both almost valueless and in huge supply. Therefore they were readily lost and when the coinage was reformed they were discarded. Studies of Roman coinage have now turned to establishing an average incidence of coins on different sorts of sites. The value lies in analysing by how much a site differs from the average in any period.

Coins have the advantage of dating themselves. Samian does not. However, if it were possible to identify a major site or sites where demand would have been relatively consistent, can the incidence of samian dated by other means show how supply varied?

A study has been made by Geoff Marsh of the Museum of London of decorated samian in London on the basis that the city would have had a relatively constant population and demand for samian would therefore have been fairly stable. Obviously London's fortune did fluctuate but this would have been nothing

49. Four sherds of plain samian cups bearing graffiti. Above is the base of a Dr 33 cup with the letters XAXI. The bottom row from left to right shows a Dr 33 wall sherd with a fish tail (?), a Dr 33 wall sherd with a backward 'N' and a Dr 27 cup with the letters IV denoting the number '4'.

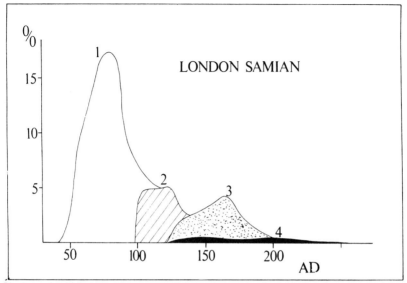

50. A graph which shows the sources of decorated samian found in London as percentages of the total by date. 1 South Gaul, 2 Les Martres-de-Veyre (Central Gaul), 3 Lezoux (Central Gaul), 4 East Gaul. (After Marsh.)

like that of a fort, subject to sudden abandonment and re-occupation. Moreover London was the major port of south-east Roman Britain throughout the period. The study concerned around 12,000 decorated samian vessels recovered from London more or less at random over the years. It is possible to calculate such a figure because decorative patterns allow sherds from different bowls to be distinguished. In theory such a group might reflect the actual rate of supply to London. Each London sherd was dated and distributed in decades. Thus a sherd dated 100-20 contributed 0.5 to the total for the decade 100-10 and 0.5 to the decade 110-20. The graph produced shows a climax of supply from South Gaul in the Flavian period and thereafter a steady decline to about 130-40 with a further small peak around 170 (figure 50).

On face value what this seems to mean is that supply was not constant, at least to south-east Britain. Either this reflects a peculiarity of supply to this area or a real variation in the rates of production at the kiln sites themselves. Evidence from other sites suggests the latter (figure 51), though some of these sites were not

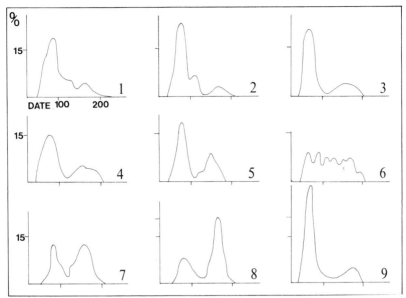

51. A series of graphs laid out in the same way as the London graph showing the comparable distribution of decorated samian in a number of other Romano-British sites. 1 London, 2 Southwark, 3 Fishbourne Palace, 4 Richborough Fort, 5 Verulamium Insula XIV, 6 Verulamium General, 7 Chester legionary fortress, 8 York legionary fortress, 9 Usk fort. (After Marsh.)

occupied continuously so occurrence of samian is affected by this as well as distribution, for example the fort at Usk. If this is correct it would therefore be completely wrong to conclude that a site which produces a great deal of South Gaulish Flavian samian, but extremely little Trajanic samian from Central Gaul, had experienced a period of decline of some sort. Some sites in Southwark have produced just this sort of samian evidence along with other evidence such as coarse wares which conversely suggest that there was a great deal of second-century activity.

Of course there are problems. It is almost impossible to be confident about changes in population, and therefore demand, in an ancient city for which we have no statistical evidence whatsoever. Changes in the province's stability may have affected the occurrence of excavated samian.

Suppose, for example, that production was more constant than suggested (or that dating is wrong). In second-century Roman Britain romanisation proceeded apace. Perhaps there was more demand beyond London for the samian which still arrived there. The incidence of re-export within Britain might serve to reduce the amount of samian on sale in second-century London, and therefore excavated in modern times.

Samian as a dating tool

It will be obvious from most of this book that samian dates are approximate only. Therefore, for example, while a number of potters are known to have worked during the period 150-200 the majority will only have been active for a couple of decades at most *within* that period. It ought, in theory, to be possible to conclude that sites, or levels, with a high proportion of the same potters' name-stamps in common were occupied roughly at the same time *within* that period, even if we do not know exactly when. This has obvious advantages for determining whether forts on the Antonine Wall and Hadrian's Wall were in operation at the same time.

This was a theory devised by B. R. Hartley in a major article and the samian name-stamp evidence supported the idea that the Antonine Wall had indeed been given up by the 160s. The principle is basically sound but it requires more data. Clearly the name-stamps are drawn from a finite number of workshops. Suppose that for the period concerned (150-200) there were about 400 Central Gaulish workshops known to have been in operation (this figure is approximately correct). At Site A we have 100 of that 400 represented. Therefore at Site B we know before we start that *any* stamp of that date has a 1 in 4 chance of being from a workshop represented at A. So, in other words, the chances of the same names turning up at B are dictated by the size of the sample you are comparing it with and the number of workshops in operation.

Clearly then the chances of name recurrence will differ for every pair of sites. The way to proceed is fairly simple. Take a major site known to have been occupied throughout the period (150-200), such as Corbridge, Northumberland, and compare it with a number of other sites also known to have been occupied throughout the period. Each one will show a rate of name recurrence that is slightly different from the theoretical. That is not important because what we want to know is the *average rate of variation from the theoretical for a site dating to 150-200.* That is the norm and only when a site of uncertain date shows a significant difference from the average figure is there reason for doubt about contemporary occupation. The theory can be applied to any period, so long as the name-stamps used are those confined to a common source.

The significance of samian

The obvious complexity inherent in understanding samian should not be interpreted as meaning that samian is incomprehensible or useless to a non-specialist. On a minor villa site half a dozen decorated sherds and a few more plain pieces may be all that turns up in the way of useful evidence. Coins are very rare on such sites. With some preparation and consideration it is possible to draw some useful 'on the spot' conclusions about the site's approximate date before submitting it to a specialist. It is all too common these days for material like samian to be carefully washed, dried and packed for a specialist's future attention, thus losing the immediate significance of the find. Are some of the sherds from the same decorated bowl? If so, is the rest of it there? Were they dispersed? If so, what caused that and is it significant for interpreting the site's history? Is it burnt? If so, was it burnt before or after being broken? Careful attention at a 1986 excavation of a villa at Sedgebrook near Plaxtol in Kent resulted in an almost complete, but very shattered, Central Gaulish Dr 37 bowl, stamped by Cinnamus, being painstakingly recovered from a clay-pit beneath a roof-fall and subsequently restored (figure 28).

Decorated samian can easily be recorded by the following means. Wrap a sheet of fine tracing paper around the sherd. Then, using a thumb, rub flaked graphite across the sherd. This will produce an image which can be glued to paper and photocopied.

As with any archaeological artefact there is no substitute for handling the material in large quantities. Obviously with samian this is rarely possible. Nevertheless it is to be hoped that this book has answered some questions and provided the basis for further study.

10
Further reading

The most obvious problems with books on samian ware are that many are out of date and many are in French or German. However, the illustrations are of considerable value in their own right so neither of these problems should be regarded as insurmountable obstacles.

General

Bémont, C., and Jacob, J. P. 'La Terre Sigillée Gallo-Romaine', *Documents d'Archéologie Française*, 6 (1986).

Déchelette, J. *Les Vases Céramiques Ornés de la Gaule Romaine*. Paris, 1904.

Hartley, B. R. 'Samian Ware or Terra Sigillata' in R. G. Collingwood and I. Richmond, *The Archaeology of Roman Britain*. Methuen, 1969.

Johns, C. *Arretine and Samian Pottery*. British Museum, 1977.

Oswald, F., and Pryce, T. D. *An Introduction to the Study of Terra-sigillata*. 1920; reprinted Gregg Press, 1965.

Webster, P. *Roman Samian Ware — Background Notes*. Department of Extra-Mural Studies, Cardiff, 1983, revised 1987.

Specialised studies

Hartley, B. R. 'The Roman Occupation of Scotland: The Evidence of Samian Ware', *Britannia*, 3 (1972), 1.

Knorr, R. *Töpfer und Fabriken verzierter Terra-Sigillata des ersten Jahrhunderts*. Stuttgart, 1919.

Knorr, R. *Terra-Sigillata-Gefässe des ersten Jahrhunderts mit Töpfernamen*. Stuttgart, 1952.

Marsh, G. 'London's Samian Supply and Its Relationship to the Development of the Gallic Samian Industry' in A. C. Anderson and A. S. Anderson (editors), *Roman Pottery Research in Britain and North West Europe*. British Archaeological Reports International Series 123, volume 1.

Oswald, F. *Index of Figure-types on Terra Sigillata, 'Samian Ware'*. 1936-7; reprinted Gregg Press, 1964.

Ricken, H. *Die Bilderschüsseln der römischen Töpfer von Rheinzabern: Tafeln*. Ludowici, Katalog VI, 1942. Plates.

Ricken H., and Fischer, C. *Die Bilderschüsseln der römischen Töpfer von Rheinzabern*. Bonn, 1963. Text.

Rogers, G. B. 'Poteries Sigillées de la Gaule Centrale, I. — Les Motifs Non Figurés,' *Gallia*, supplement 28 (1974).

Stanfield, J. A., and Simpson, G. *Central Gaulish Potters*. Oxford University Press, 1958.

Terrisse, J. R. 'Les Céramiques sigillées Gallo-Romaines des Martres-de-Veyre', *Gallia*, supplement 19 (1968).

Samian reports

Atkinson, D. 'A Hoard of Samian Ware from Pompeii', *Journal of Roman Studies*, 4 (1914), 26-64.

Atkinson, D. *Report on Excavations at Wroxeter (the Roman City of Viroconium) in the County of Salop, 1923-27.* Birmingham, 1942.

Bird, J., in L. Miller, J. Schofield and M. Rhodes (editors), *The Roman Quay at St Magnus House, London. Excavations at New Fresh Wharf, Lower Thames Street, London 1974-78,* special paper number 8 of the London and Middlesex Archaeological Society, 1986.

Dannell, G. B., in B. Cunliffe, *Excavations at Fishbourne, Volume 2 — The Finds.* Society of Antiquaries Research Report, 1971.

De la Bédoyère, G. *The Roman Site at Billingsgate Lorry Park, London — A Catalogue of the Samian and Other Finds.* British Archaeological Reports (British Series) 154, 1986.

Dore, J. N., and Gillam, J. P. *The Roman Fort at South Shields 1875-1975.* Society of Antiquaries of Newcastle upon Tyne, 1979.

Hartley, B. R., and Dickinson, B., in S. S. Frere, *Verulamium Excavations,* volumes I and III. Society of Antiquaries Research Report, 1972, and Oxford University Committee for Archaeology, 1984.

Hawkes, C. F. C., and Hull, M. R. *Camulodunum.* Society of Antiquaries Research Report, 1947.

Hull, M. R. *The Potters' Kilns of Roman Colchester.* Society of Antiquaries Research Report, 1963.

Simpson, G. 'The Aldgate Potter: A Maker of Romano-British Samian Ware', *Journal of Roman Studies,* 42 (1952).

Smith, R. A. 'On the Wreck on Pudding Pan Rock, Herne Bay, Kent, and on the Gallo-Roman Red Ware Recently Recovered from the Rock', *Proceedings of the Society of Antiquaries of London,* second series, 21 and 22, 1905-7 and 1907-9.

Webster, P. V. 'More British Samian by the Aldgate-Pulborough Potter', *Britannia,* 6 (1975).

11
Museums

As an almost ubiquitous Romano-British site find, samian ware will be found in most associated museums in Britain. However, as with most collections of pottery the vast majority is stored and only the best representative examples are displayed. This is sufficient for most interests, while access to the remainder is normally possible for serious students seeking specific information.

British Museum, Great Russell Street, London WC1B 3DG. Telephone: 01-636 1555.

Carlisle Museum and Art Gallery, Tullie House, Castle Street, Carlisle, Cumbria CA3 8TP. Telephone: Carlisle (0228) 34781.

Castle Museum, Norwich NR1 3JU. Telephone: Norwich (0603) 611277.

Colchester and Essex Museum, The Castle, Colchester, Essex CO1 1TJ. Telephone: Colchester (0206) 712490.

Corinium Museum, Park Street, Cirencester, Gloucestershire GL7 2BX. Telephone: Cirencester (0285) 5611.

Dorset County Museum, High West Street, Dorchester, Dorset DT1 1XA. Telephone: Dorchester (0305) 62735.

Gloucester City Museum and Art Gallery, Brunswick Road, Gloucester GL1 1HP. Telephone: Gloucester (0452) 24131.

Grosvenor Museum, 27 Grosvenor Street, Chester CH1 2DD. Telephone: Chester (0244) 316944.

Jewry Wall Museum of Archaeology, St Nicholas Circle, Leicester. Telephone: Leicester (0533) 554100.

Lincoln City and County Museum, Broadgate, Lincoln LN2 1HQ. Telephone: Lincoln (0522) 30401.

Museum of Antiquities of the University and the Society of Antiquaries of Newcastle upon Tyne, The University, Newcastle upon Tyne NE1 7RU. Telephone: Tyneside (091) 2328511 extensions 3844 and 3849.

Museum of London, London Wall, London EC2Y 5HN. Telephone: 01-600 3699.

National Museum of Wales, Cathays Park, Cardiff CF1 3ND. Telephone: Cardiff (0222) 397951.

Reading Museum and Art Gallery, Blagrave Street, Reading RG1 1QH. Telephone: Reading (0734) 55911. (Silchester.)

Rowley's House Museum, Barker Street, Shrewsbury, Shropshire SY1 1QT. Telephone: Shrewsbury (0743) 61196.

Royal Museum and Art Gallery, High Street, Canterbury, Kent CT1 2JE. Telephone: Canterbury (0227) 452747.

Royal Museum of Scotland, Queen Street, Edinburgh EH2 1JD. Telephone: 031-225 7534.

Verulamium Museum, St Michael's, St Albans, Hertfordshire AL3 4SW. Telephone: St Albans (0727) 54659.

Yorkshire Museum, Museum Gardens, York YO1 2DR. Telephone: York (0904) 29745.

Index

Page numbers in italic refer to illustrations